To all the children, grandchildren and great grandchildren of Tsuneko Hongo

Table of Contents

Preface

Masanori Hongo

The Making of This Book

The editing of this poetry book, by my mother, was an experience I never before encountered – ten different dictionaries, resource books on horticulture and hymnals, Internet research, and discussions and meetings with many individuals. It was an eye opener for me to understand that she had such love for poetry, family, and all other aspect of life.

The journey towards the creation of this book began over a century ago with the birth of my mother. When my mother passed away in 1968, my father and my mother's Ginushisha (Silver Rain) poetry club friends created the original Japanese language version of the book. Approximately 27 years later, my sister Hatsue took on the initial project of having the book translated to English and compiled into a nearly completed new book.

Upon my sister's passing, I took over the project and began working on it in earnest during the spring of 2004. The final project team and I took the whole thing apart and painstakingly put it together again in the form presented here. This barely begins to describe all of the hard work and tough discussions that went into making sure that every last poem was translated as best as we could and every part of the book was just right. Through much pushing and pulling, we kept our focus on creating something that would be presentable and do justice to my mother's poetry.

My General Thoughts

Whenever I left home I always wondered when I would return. Work, school, internment camps, and military service kept me away from home and my mother for over one fifth of her life.

The longest stretch of time I spent away from home was during a five-year period. It lasted from before the war began up to a ten-day visit I had right before I entered the service. My month and a half arduous odyssey from an Internment Camp to Chicago, and on to Hilo, Hawaii was a testament to my desire to get home. No obstacle was too great as I begged and petitioned my way for transportation to cross half a continent and half an ocean to get home. Working on this book brought back so many pleasurable memories that this too was like a homecoming.

Looking back, my mother, as an Issei (first generation), was an exceptional woman - educated in a missionary school, she was able to read and write both Japanese and English, and could play piano too. Mother led by example without any harsh words for us and always encouraged us in all our pursuits. One thing that sticks in my mind is that she wore with pride a WCTU (Women Christian Temperance Union) pin, but never told anyone not to drink alcohol – she led by example and conviction as a Christian.

Like most of us, we often take our parents for granted and don't think deeply about their many talents and about their lives. Working on this book was a most welcome challenge because it helped to reacquaint me with my mother. She had more depth and breadth about life and substance than I ever imagined. The wonderful lessons of her life kept me going to the completion of this project.

My mother's poetry and the included information in the back of the book are part of my family's history. In my small way this tanka book is for my mother and all the generations before us who made it possible to be where we are and who we are today.

This project had many contributors. We were almost like the petals of a vanda orchid. Our final project team was the last petal that made this beautiful book possible.

Here are the people that accompanied me on the last leg of this great journey – Miyako Sueyoshi (translation editing), Leonard Chan (editing and book layout), Philip Chin (editing), Jean Chan (cover and incidental art design), Florence Hongo (moral support), and last but not least my brother-in-law, Harry Kawamoto, for graciously donating financial support to complete the project that my sister Hatsue started.

The Managers of Ginushisha,
Zenko Matayoshi and Tetsuo Yukawa

(This is the preface that appeared in Kurenai Hongo's original Japanese version of this poetry book. It has since been translated into English for its inclusion in *Petals of the Vanda*.)

Kurenai Hongo's poetry history is quite long. Her poems are highly refined in style and decency. Her whole life was based on religious conviction. She was a loving wife, and good mother to her children. She was deeply loved by her grandchildren. The Christian home she made was certainly highly respected by all.

Her long-suffering illness was to her another step of joy towards the glory of God. She never questioned God about her suffering.

Kurenai-san was always present at Dr. Matayoshi's living room to attend the monthly poetry meetings. After her illness we could no longer see her at her favorite seat under the window relaxing on the sofa so comfortably. How transient life is to think that she has left us so completely.

It was discovered recently that she had left a will which must have been written during her suffering as she was ready to welcome her death. This will was found in an unexpected place.

By the ardent request of Kurenai-san's husband Torakiyo-san, Ginushisha poetry group endeavored to accept this task and are now ready to present this book to you. It consists of her will, and over one hundred poems selected from among the poems composed since 1963 as Kurenai.

Mrs. Hongo was raised to heaven on November 20, 1968 at Kuakini Hospital in Honolulu watched over by her husband, sons and daughter. On the 21st, her body was cremated at Hosoi undertaker's and the prayer service was held at Nuuanu church led by the Rev. Sutekichi Osumi and Rev. Kiei Endo. Many friends were present to bid farewell and to see her off on the 22nd to Hilo.

The following day, on the 23rd, at five o'clock in the evening, the funeral service was held by Rev. Frederick Hyslop and Rev. Tosuke Ohta at Holy Cross Church. The church was filled and the funeral was such an inspiring experience that we, her close friends, were soothed and felt reassured (for our loss.)

Further, we should like to add our gratitude to Yoshiko Ohta in her cooperation to publish this book of poetry.

Foreward

Garrett Hongo, Professor of Poetry and Author of *Volcano: A Memoir of Hawai`i*

Petals of the Vanda comes as a marvelous revelation and verse letter from the past. It is the collection of *tanka* from Kurenai, the pen-name of my own grand-aunt Tsuneko Hongo, and commemorates a worthy life full of joy, reflection, and a love for poetry.

Celebrated are ephemeral and yet glorious moments of daily life—the arrival of a bunch of flowers from her son far away, holding the hands and gazing into the face of an old friend, an article in the local paper mentioning that a grandchild has just won a prize, and many scenes of travel to Japan and California and homecomings to Hilo.

Throughout, there is the classic elegance of expression inherent in the language of the *tanka*, an older form than the *haiku* and more dignified, even restrained, capable of rendering delicate emotions, fleeting moods of wonder and delight, great sadness.

I was very moved and delighted by the collection's sentiments and forms, reading the Japanese out loud to myself, marveling at its sophistication and discipline, its care for allowing words to fall in just the right rhythms. I love tanka, and I love these even more because of all the connections to Hawaii, our common past, and the new diasporic culture that generation was building. I find the poems tender and full of humanity, a love of family and community, appreciations of nature. They strike me as very "Japanese" and representative of a hopeful, momentous time in our past. They are like the turning of colors on the petal of a plumeria blossom—white to brilliant crimson—unforgettably graceful and beautiful.

Introduction

Hatsue Hongo Kawamoto,
Honolulu, Hawaii, March, 1995

The poems in this modest volume are truly Mother's gift to her children and grandchildren, whom she loved dearly.

When Mother passed away in 1968 at the age of 79, she left behind hundreds of poems. Several members of Mother's Ginushisha (Silver Rain) poetry club in Hilo, approached Dad to publish a book of Mother's poems because her poems were thought to be of such fine quality and that if not published at that time they would be forgotten forever.

A few members of the poetry club selected those poems which they thought would make a fitting memorial book. The title "*Vanda no Hanabira*" (*Petals of the Vanda*) was chosen because at one time the Hongo family was a commercial grower of the lovely vanda orchid. Mother's pen name was "Kurenai" meaning "Crimson."

Dad took these poems to Japan and through a relative found a printer who volunteered to organize the poems and publish a limited number of 200 copies. These were given as a memorial gift to family, church friends in Hilo and relatives in Japan.

With the coming of the next and additional generations who could not read Japanese, again and again I heard Dad say, "How pitiful that my children are not able to read and appreciate Mother's poems."

When I visited my cousin Shizue Oka (Mother's sister's daughter) in Osaka, I asked her to translate Mother's "Vanda no Hanabira." Her relationship with Mother was close and she knew Mother's inner spirit well. She was happy to undertake the project.

Translations are difficult because true meaning of words cannot be transposed precisely from one language to another. Furthermore, many terms in the Japanese language are not found in the English language. Therefore, some of the delicate nuances of the original writing are lost.

Knowing this, Shizue Oka did her utmost in translating, keeping in mind Mother's spirit and soul.

Mother wrote tanka (also known as waka), an ancient Japanese poetry form written in 31 syllables—5,7,5,7,7. For example:

Usubi sasu(5)   asa no niwamo ni(7)   furu ame no(5)
hosoku hikareru(7)   nangoku no aki(7)

One or two syllables may be added to the traditional 31 syllables. The entire poem contains 12 to 20 words.

Tanka captures the fragile quality of beauty and emotion of a particular moment. The poems are true expressions of the heart and are written on the spur of the moment. Thus, tanka are pure, simple, spontaneous creations, and yet they have a depth of subtle meaning. When too much thought goes into writing a tanka, it is no longer an expression of the true self, and it is therefore not a true tanka.

When Mother was raising her family, she had little time for herself. Most of the poems herein were written after the children grew up and left home. Whenever a tanka came to her mind, she would quickly drop whatever she was doing, be it sewing, gardening, or hanging the laundry. Knowing how fragile and fleeting were her thoughts, she would quickly go to her writing drawer and write the tanka in her writing pad or on a piece of paper before her treasured image would escape her forever.

Mother's love for literature began early in life. While she was in college (Aoyama Gakuin, Tokyo), she majored in literature. Her teachers were American missionary educators. When I was studying Shakespeare in high school, I remember being amazed because Mother recalled from memory passages from the "Merchant of Venice." In her youth, she was also under the tutelage of a master poet from whom she learned to refine her writing of tanka.

Through Mother's tanka, now translated, edited, and finally produced into a book form, she has left a precious legacy for her children, grandchildren and succeeding generations to enjoy and to get to know the spirit of this special person.

Chapter One
Home Country

Chapter 1 – Home Country

Oh, the taste and the fragrance of our home country
How our hearts leap to open the parcel

ふるさとの　味と香りの　小包を　ときて我らの　心おどりぬ

Furusato no   aji to kaori no   kozutsumi o
tokite warera no   kokoro odorinu

❀

From Japan came origami
And look how the children of all nations delight in this art

日本より　来りし技（わざ）の　折紙に　各国人の　子ら興ずるも

Nihon yori   kitarishi waza no   origami ni
kakukokujin no   kora kyozurumo

❀

The deep tender dignity of my home country
Is felt in the arrangement of the daffodils
In contrast with a branch of a pine tree

ふるさとの　情緒豊かに　主体なる　松にそえたる　水仙の花

Furusato no   jocho yutakani   shutainaru
matsu ni soetaru   suisen no hana

As I hold the paper crafted tea caddy
I appreciate the warmth of my home country's heart

ふるさとの　あたたかき心　こもりたる　手もみの茶入れ　なつかしみをり

Furusato no   atatakaki kokoro   komoritaru
temomi no chaire   natsukashimiori

❀

As I listen and watch the TV program from Tokyo
I feel as if I'm walking along the streets of Yurakucho

東都よりの　生放送に　きき入りつ　見入りつ我も　有楽町をゆく

Toto yori no   nama hoso ni   kikiiritsu
miiritsu ware mo   Yurakucho o yuku

❀

Violets I had picked under the cherry blossoms
Oh, those lovely spring days at Koganei are now far, far away

小金井の　桜の下に　すみれつみし　のどけき春も　遠くなりけり

Koganei no   sakura no shita ni   sumire tsumishi
nodokeki haru mo   tokunarikeri

Chapter 1 – Home Country

Chapter Two
Grandchildren

Chapter 2 – Grandchildren

Full of life in growth
Our grandchildren soar notes of jubilant joy

豊にも　生命のびゆく　孫等の上に　高らかに湧く　歓喜の調

Yutakani mo　inochi nobiyuku　magora no ue ni
takarakani waku　kanki no shirabe

❀

Listening to my grandchild play the Moonlight Sonata
The days of my youth flash back to me

孫のひく　月光の曲　聞きおりて　我若き日を　ふと思ひ出ぬ

Mago no hiku　Gekko no Kyoku (Moonlight Sonata)　kikiorite
waga wakaki hi o　futo omoidenu

❀

I've reached such an age our topics when we meet are about
One's grandchildren and our declining health

相寄れば　孫の話と　みづからの　おとろへ語る　年とはなりぬ

Aiyoreba　mago no hanashi to　mizukara no
otoroe kataru　toshi to wa narinu

I'm sewing a dress for my grandchild who is leaving for school in Honolulu
How light is the needle and my heart so happy

ホノルルの　学窓にゆく　孫の衣を　縫ふ針かるく　心たのしも

Honolulu no   gakuso ni yuku   mago no i o
nuu hari karuku   kokoro tanoshimo

❀

May your days be happy
Please live a long life is my grandchild's dearest desire

楽々と　日日を過して　長命を　得て給はれと　孫の切願

Rakurakuto   hibi o sugoshite   chomei o
ete tamaware to   mago no setsugan

❀

Wearing the white plumeria lei
Great must be our granddaughter's triumph dancing the hula

純白の　ブルメリアレイ　首にかけ　フラおどりする　孫の得意さ

Junpaku no   plumeria lei   kubi ni kake
hula odorisuru   mago no tokuisa

Chapter 2 – Grandchildren

Consoled by the hearty love of my grandchildren
I live in tears of happiness

孫たちの　やさしき心の　いたはりに　涙ぐましき　幸に生きゐる

Magotachi no　yasashiki kokoro no　itawari ni
namidagumashiki　sachi ni ikiiru

✿

At the sound of the airplane[1], our little grandchild puts his finger up
He points down, the dog barks - how cute of him

幼き孫　飛行機の音に　指を上げ　犬ほえば下指す　愛らしき機智

Osanaki mago　hikoki no oto ni　yubi o age
inu hoeba shita sasu　airashiki kichi

✿

Our grandchild welcomed us home
A surprise present greets us, a glistening Christmas tree

留守のまに　サプライズプレゼント　孫のたてし　クリスマスツリ
かがやきてあり

Rusu no ma ni　surprise present　mago no tateshi
Christmas tree　kagayakite ari

---

[1] Home was located close to the airport

Thrilled by the flattering letter of my grandchild
Busily I sew the muumuu she asks for

たどたどしき　孫のたよりを　喜びて　ほしきムームーを　急ぎぬひ居り

Tadotadoshiki　mago no tayori o　yorokobite
hoshiki mu-mu o　isogi nuiori

❀

At the pond my grandchild scoops killifish[2]
His excited call roused me from my daydream

池の辺に　めだかすくひて　孫よべば　はずみし声に　夢やぶられぬ

Ike no be ni　medaka sukuite　mago yobeba
hazumishi koe ni　yume yaburarenu

❀

To my call "take picture!"
My little grandchild tugs his doggie along, he takes the picture with him

「テークピッチャー」と　一言言へば　幼な孫　犬ひきつれて　ポーズつくるも

"Take picture!" to　hitokoto ieba　osana mago
inu hikitsurete　pose tsukurumo

---

[2] Mosquito fish

Chapter 2 – Grandchildren

"Grandma, sew me this style!"
She hands me a picture she drew, oh how innocent it is

グランマよ　此スタイルを　縫ひてよと　孫のえがきし　絵のあどけなさ

Grandma yo　kono style o　nuite yo to
mago no egakishi　e no adokenasa

❀

A gift from Honolulu my grandchild hands me
A teacup, ah what colorful charming design!

ホノルルの　みやげと孫の　持ちくれし　湯呑の模様　あでやかにして

Honolulu no　miyage to mago no　mochikureshi
yunomi no moyo　adeyakanishite

❀

A sickly being as I am, I have outlived my mother's age
Here I live consoled by my grandchild's loving care

ひよわき身も　母みまかりし　年を過ぎ　孫のやさしき　いたはりに生く

Hiyowaki mi mo　haha mimakarishi　toshi o sugi
mago no yasashiki　itawarini iku

Our grandchild won the blue ribbon for an article in the newspaper
We rejoice over it together with him

新聞科の　大会に出て　特賞を　孫の得たるを　共に喜ぶ

Shinbunka no　taikai ni dete　tokusho o
mago no etaru o　tomo ni yorokobu

Chapter 2 – Grandchildren

Chapter Three
Flowers

As the sky clears I step out on the ground
To see the orchids afresh in the joy of spring
Vie with each other in full bloom

晴まみて　地に下りたてば　蘭の花　競ひ出づるに　喜びの湧く

Haremamite　chi ni oritateba　ran no hana
kisoi izuru ni　yorokobi no waku

❀

The garden is lovely with iris in full bloom
The purer the white, the lovelier still - oh this young summer morning

あやめさく　庭は美し　ましろなる　色はなほよし　初夏の朝

Ayame saku　niwa wa utsukushi　mashironaru
iro wa nao yoshi　hatsunatsu no asa

❀

High up among the branches cluster the African tulips
My eyes are fixed on the fascinating vermilion

梢高く　むれさくアフリカン　チューリップ　思はず見はる　朱のあざやかさ

Kozue takaku　muresaku African　tulip
omowazu miharu　shu no azayakasa

Have they come from Africa?
This facinating tree with poisonous flowers, in brilliant flaming blooms

アフリカより　来りし花か　毒もちて　いとあでやかに　咲く火焔木

Africa yori　kitarishi hana ka　doku mochite
ito adeyakani　saku kaenboku

❀

Her sweet scent so modest
The plumeria with dignity, she truly is the Princess of Flowers

かすかなる　かをりもゆかし　プルメリア　気品も高し　花の王女か

Kasukanaru　kaori mo yukashi　plumeria
kihin mo takashi　hana no ojo ka

❀

The scattered plumeria blossoms beautify the lawn
Her lightish pink setting off the green grass

ブルメリア　散りて芝生を　飾りをり　うす紅色の　緑にはえて

Plumeria　chirite shibafu o　kazariori
usubeniiro no　midori ni haete

Chapter 3 – Flowers

In this beautiful paradise of flowers
I dream day after day of planting trees - this is my wish these days

美しき　花の天国　夢みつつ　日毎植樹に　はげむ此の頃

Utsukushiki　hana no tengoku　yume-mitsutsu
higoto shokuju ni　hagemu konogoro

❀

In the late fall along the Kona road
The poinsettia vie with each other in colors red, yellow, and white

晩秋の　コナ路をゆけば　ポインセチアの　赤黄白と　色の競演

Banshu no　Kona-ji o yukeba　poinsettia no
aka ki shiro to　iro no kyoen

❀

The cymbidium bloom, dignified in the cold
Proudly befitting the Princess of Orchids

気品高く　蘭の王女と　ほこるげに　冷寒に咲く　シンビディウムの花

Kihin takaku　ran no ojo to　hokorugeni
reikan ni saku　cymbidium no hana

Through the wide picture window
I see an apple tree, with white blossoms flowering and also green fruits

大窓に　絵の如うつる　リンゴの木　白き花さき　青き実も見ゆ

Omado ni　e no goto utsuru　ringo no ki
shiroki hana saki　aoki mi mo miyu

❁

In a nook among the weeds
Bloom amaryllis in scarlet flames, so marvelous a sight to see

片隅の　雑草の中に　アマリリス　燃ゆる緋色に　咲ける驚き

Katasumi no　zasso no naka ni　amaryllis
moyuru hiiro ni　sakeru odoroki

❁

After sweating over the weeds
I take a shower, how refreshed I feel (in and out), with a brimfull of vigor

草にいどみ　流せし汗に　シャワーとれば　さわやかの気の　心身にみつ

Kusa ni idomi　nagaseshi ase ni　shower toreba
sawayakano ki no　shinshin ni mitsu

Chapter 3 – Flowers

The coconut avenue is so beautiful
Standing against the glowing sunset,
bathing their backs in the flaming light

燃ゆる如き　夕映の光　背にうけて　立ちゐる椰子の　並木美し

Moyuru gotoki　yubae no hikari　se ni ukete
tachiiru yashi no　namiki utsukushi

❀

As autumn deepens, the clustering berries color
This arouses in me a feeling that I am pressed for time

秋深み　群れおるベリーの　色づけば　何とはなしに　心いそぐも

Aki fukami　mureoru berry no　irozukeba
nan to wa nashi ni　kokoro isogumo

❀

In my long absence the orchid waited for me in the house
Now, it greets me with an abundance of lovely flowers

長き日を　留守居せし蘭　愛らしき　花あまたつけ　我によびかく

Nagaki hi o　rusuiseshi ran　airashiki
hana amata tsuke　ware ni yobi kaku

In the bright sun there is movement
People picking flowers in the fields, caressed by a breeze

もの皆は　光の中に　動きをり　花つむ人も　風なづる畑も

Mono mina wa　hikari no naka ni　ugokiori
hana tsumu hito mo　kaze nazuru hata mo

❀

Even in these long days of the tropics, spring is here
I see a floral arrangement of pretty peach blossoms

常夏の　郷（さと）とはいえど　春なれや　愛らしき桃の　花活けてをり

Tokonatsu no　sato to wa iedo　haru nareya
airashiki momo no　hana iketeori

❀

To the picture of her, I offer chrysanthemums that I raised
I can hear mother's sweet words come back to me

うつしえに　手植の薫菊　手向けつつ　やさしき母の　言葉思えり

Utsushie ni　teue no kungiku　tamuketsutsu
yasashiki haha no　kotoba omoeri

The pine branch with the glorious pink camellia
This arrangement heralds the joy of the New Year

松ヶ枝（え）に　乙女椿を　あしらひし　生花に春の　寿ぎてあり

Matsuga e ni　otometsubaki o　ashiraishi
seika ni haru no　kotohogiteari

❀

Mango blossoms in chorus bloom
Singing the song of spring

春の歌　うたふが如く　一せいに　マンゴの花の　咲きみちてをり

Haru no uta　utau ga gotoku　issei ni
mango no hana no　sakimichite ori

❀

The chibochina blooms gorgeously
Expressing my joy, whether she knows it or not

チボチナの　花あでやかに　咲きつげり　我の喜び　知るや知らずや

Chibochina no　hana adeyakani　saki-tsugeri
ware no yorokobi　shiruya shirazuya

I took you away from the (mother) root dear uzura
Flourish with your new master in Hilo

根分せし　ウズラの花よ　新らしき　ヒロの主人と　共に栄えよ

Newakeseshi　uzura no hana yo　atarashiki
Hilo no shujin to　tomo ni sakaeyo

❀

At the other place the uzura flower did not bloom for a long time
Replanted here at Hilo it bloomed with beautiful flowers

彼の地にて　長く開かぬ　ウズラ花　ヒロにうつして　美しく咲く

Ka no chi ni te　nagaku hirakanu　uzurabana
Hilo ni utsushite　utsukushiku saku

❀

When my eyes glanced at the uzura flower
The warmth of friendship circles in my heart

ウズラ花　ながむるごとに　あたたかき　友の情の　胸にゆきかう

Uzurabana　nagamurugoto ni　atatakaki
tomo no nasake no　mune ni yukikau

Chapter 3 – Flowers

Hail to the clear mid-summer sky
The crepe myrtle beautifully blooms

晴れ渡る　真夏の空に　呼応して　百日紅の花　あでやかに咲く

Harewataru　manatsu no sora ni　kooshite
sarusuberi no hana　adeyakani saku

Chapter Four
Birds

The cardinals' praise of nature's love
Echoes to heaven and earth again this morning

今朝もまた　自然の愛を　讃美する　紅鳥の声　天地に響く

Kesa mo mata　shizen no ai o　sanbisuru
benidori no koe　tenchi ni hibiku

❀

God gives to the frail little birds
The twinkling sound of a silver bell

銀鈴を　うちふる如き　響をば　か細き鳥に　備へます神

Ginrei o　uchifurugotoki　hibikioba
kabosoki tori ni　sonae masu kami

❀

Walking through the path of ferns and singing birds
Even the air is sweet, so says my guest

しだ茂り　小鳥さえづる　道ゆけば　空気も甘しと　客人のいふ

Shida shigeri　kotori saezuru　michi yukeba
kuki mo amashi to　kyakubito no iu

Breaking the quiet, clear morning air
The lovely birds begin their fall contest

晴渡る　朝の沈黙（しじま）を　やぶるがに　愛（かな）しき鳥の　秋の競演

Harewataru　asa no shijima o　yaburugani
kanashiki tori no　aki no kyoen

From the window we set free our long cherished bird
As she leaves the nest of her first born baby

長き年　愛せし小鳥　放ちやり　窓辺に初児（ういご）の　床しつらひぬ

Nagaki toshi　aiseshi kotori　hanachiyari
madobe ni uigo no　toko shitsurainu

Chapter 4 – Birds

Chapter Five
Friends

Chapter 5 – Friends

I welcomed a friend to Hilo
Who promised in Tokyo to visit Hawaii, how extremely happy was I

東都にて　ハワイを訪うと　云ひし友　ヒロにむかえて　うれしさ極む

Toto ni te   Hawaii o tou to   iishi tomo
Hilo ni mukaete   ureshisa kiwamu

❁

Praising the magnificent nature of the island
My friend was happy with the lei I gave her on departure

雄大なる　島の自然を　ほめちぎり　レイを喜び　友は去りゆきし

Yudainaru   shima no shizen o   homechigiri
lei o yorokobi   tomo wa sariyukishi

❁

Where the great tidal wave took my friend's life
Tall grass is now growing on that land

大つなみ　おそいて友の　命まで　とられし地にも　草高く茂げる

Otsunami   osoite tomo no   inochi made
torareshi chi ni mo   kusa takaku shigeru

Every time I read the message of condolence at a friend's funeral
I deeply realize that I also am expected there

親しみし　友への弔詞　読む毎に　待たるる身とぞ　しみじみ思ふ

Shitashimishi　tomo e no choji　yomu goto ni
mataruru mi to zo　shimijimi omu

❀

Among the collection of letters are my friend's prayers for my recovery
My eyes moisten at their tender feelings

いえよとの　祈をこめし　寄せ書きの　友の情に　ただ涙しぬ

Ieyo to no　inori o komeshi　yosegaki no
tomo no nasake ni　tada namidashinu

❀

Healed through my friends' prayers
I rejoice as songs well up in my heart again

友どちの　深き祈りに　病いえ　歌う心の　湧くもうれしき

Tomodachi no　fukaki inori ni　yamai ie
utau kokoro no　wakumo ureshiki

Chapter 5 – Friends

Here in Honolulu there is so much joy
At meeting a dear friend, after a long separation

久々に　親しき友に　会ふといふ　喜多し　ここホノルルは

Hisabisani　shitashiki tomo ni　au to iu
yorokobi ooshi　koko Honolulu wa

❀

Close to her nineties, my friend takes pride in flying
Hither to the Mainland and thither to Japan

九十路に　近き我友　大陸に　日本にと飛び　ほこりおるかも

Kyujuji ni　chikaki waga tomo　tairiku ni
Nippon ni to tobi　hokoriorukamo

❀

In my joy of recovery
Raises in my mind, the love and care of my friends

病いえし　喜の中に　数多き　友の恩愛　胸にせまるも

Yamai ieshi　yorokobi no uchi ni　kazu ooki
tomo no onai　mune ni semarumo

The death of a friend
Reveals that my life is full of repentance in my closing years

悔多き　我生涯も　終焉に　近づきたりと　友の死は告ぐ

Kui ooki　waga shogai mo　shuen ni
chikazukitari to　tomo no shi wa tsugu

❀

I am lonely and yearn for my friend
Whose going away has turned her two poems into her last gift of memory

かたみとも　いふべき二首の　歌残し　友ゆきましぬ　淋しなつかし

Katami to mo　iubeki nishu no　uta nokoshi
tomo yukimashinu　sabishi natsukashi

❀

On the way to Kona
My alma mater friend cries with joy at the flame red poinsettia[3]

同窓の　友はコナ路の　ポインセティアの　燃ゆる真紅に　歓声をあぐ

Doso no　tomo wa Kona ji no　poinsettia no
moyuru shinku ni　kansei o agu

---

[3] They grow in hedges six feet high

Chapter 5 – Friends

As we welcome two friends from Tokyo
Our house swells in the excitement of our beloved reunion

友二人　東都より来て　我家は　なつかしき気の　みちあふれおり

Tomo futari　toto yori kite　waga ie wa
natsukashiki ki no　michiafureori

❀

Many of our friends have passed away
But we rejoice, as the rest of us being here together

他界せし　友多き中に　我らよく　ここに会ひ得しを　喜びあへり

Takaiseshi　tomo ooki naka ni　warera yoku
kokoni aieshi o　yorokobiaeri

❀

Pineapple, mango, papaya, and lichee
My friend is enchanted and relishes the flavor of the sub-tropics

パインアップル　マンゴ　パパイア　ライチーと　南国の味に　友は魅せらる

Pineapple,　mango, papaya,　lichee to
nangoku no aji ni　tomo wa miseraru

My friend's house is built in the Maui highland
I am awakened by the neighs of the horses and moos of the cows

友の家は　マウイ高原に　たちてあり　馬のいななき　牛の声に醒む

Tomo no ie wa　Maui kogen ni　tachite ari
uma no inanaki　ushi no koe ni samu

❀

I met a friend, although I could not remember her name
We lovingly chat away

町角に　会ひし人の名　忘れしまま　ただなつかしく　語りあひたり

Machikado ni　aishi hito no na　wasureshi mama
tada natsukashiku　katariaitari

❀

The matsutake my friend picked
Gives forth its fragrance to this house like the morning of late fall

友の手にて　とりし松茸　我家に　香りはなちぬ　晩秋の朝

Tomo no te ni te　torishi matsutake　waga ie ni
kaori hanachinu　banshu no asa

Chapter 5 – Friends

I take my friend's hands from California and we gaze into each other's face
It's like a dream come true

夢の如き　真なりとて　手をとりぬ　加州より来し　友と相見て

Yume no gotoki　makotonari to te　te o torinu
Kashu yori koshi　tomo to aimite

❀

I take mornings walks with my friend
Happily, singing songs as we go along, arm in arm

朝夕の　散歩に友と　うでをくみ　歌うたひつつ　たのしくゆきぬ

Asayu no　sanpo ni tomo to　ude o kumi
uta utaitsutsu　tanoshiku yukinu

❀

As my friend plays her organ
We sing our songs full of deep memories

友の弾く　オルガンの音に　あはせつつ　思出ふかき　歌をうたへり

Tomo no hiku　organ no ne ni　awasetsutsu
omoide fukaki　uta o utaeri

My dear classmate sends cherished matsutake
Oh how they scented the whole house

友情を　のせて飛び来し　松茸の　香り我家に　みちみちてをり

Yujo o　nosete tobikoshi　matsutake no
kaori wagaya ni　michimichiteori

❀

Of the fifty year old stories of the past
It seems like only yesterday, to hear my friend speak

五十年の　昔語りとは　思はれず　昨日の如く　友は語れる

Gojunen no　mukashigatari to wa　omoware zu
kino no gotoku　tomo wa katareru

❀

Thinking of you my heart is filled with joy
I am deeply impressed for you to receive the highest honor[4]

最高の　ほまれをうけし　感激の　君を思ひて　嬉しさ極む（又吉姉に）

Saiko no　homare o ukeshi　kangeki no
kimi o omoite　ureshisa kiwamu

---

[4] Friend – Mrs. Matayoshi

Chapter 5 – Friends

Chapter Six
Children

Chapter 6 – Children

From San Francisco my son sent
Pussy willows, peach blossoms, and red roses
Oh my heart dances with delight!

桑港の　子より送りし　猫柳　桃紅ばらと　心おどるも

Soko no　ko yori okurishi　nekoyanagi
momo benibara to　kokoro odorumo

❀

When I finish school, my heart's content, I'll succeed too
So saying our son shaking his arms

学窓を　巣立たば我も　思ふまま　ためさんものと　かひなふる子よ

Gakuso o　sudataba ware mo　omoumama
tamesan mono to　kaina furu ko yo

❀

May the child offer true service to people and the world
Thus this grandmother prays

世に人に　まことの奉仕　いたす子と　ならまほしとぞ　祈る此婆

Yo ni hito ni　makoto no hoshi　itasu ko to
naramahoshi to zo　inoru kono baba

With no children engaged in heated arguments
We eat our New Year mochi soup at a corner of the table

口論に　花を咲かせし　子等もなく　食卓の隅に　雑煮たぶるも

Koron ni　hana o sakaseshi　kora mo naku
shokutaku no sumi ni　zoni taburumo

❀

Celebrating their father's 77th birthday
The children sent yellow chrysanthemums
On his desk I arrange the flowers

父親の　喜の字の祝と　子等くれし　デスクの上に　黄菊かざりぬ

Chichioya no　kinoji no iwai to　kora kureshi
desk no ue ni　kigiku kazarinu

❀

Children with grandchildren gathered to celebrate
Papa's eightieth birthday to our great joy

父親の　八十の誕生　祝ふとて　子孫より来し　大いなる感激

Chichioya no　hachiju no tanjo　iwautote
ko mago yori kishi　oinaru kangeki

Chapter 6 – Children

Such frequent correspondence between mother and daughter
How could you have so much to write about, wonders daddy

いとしげく　母娘（ははこ）の交はす　文通に　書く種よくも　あるといふ父

Ito shigeku　hahako no kawasu　buntsu ni
kaku tane yoku mo　aru to iu chichi

❀

When I think of mothers
Whose husbands and sons are away in the battlefields
The New Year hesitates deep in gloom

夫や子を　戦野におくれる　人思ひ　新春もなほ　暗くよどめり

Otto ya ko o　senya ni okureru　hito omoi
shinshun mo nao　kuraku yodomeri

❀

Wearing the muumuu I sewed with the cloth my daughter gave me
Happily I walked along the city streets

娘（こ）のくれし　布にて縫ひし　ムームーを　まといて街を　はればれとゆく

Ko no kureshi　nuno ni te nuishi　mu-mu o
matoite machi o　harebare to yuku

Praying God's blessing on Mother's Day
The card from my daughter warms my heart

神の祝福　母の上にと　祈る娘の　カードに見入り　胸あたたかし（母の日に）

Kami no shukufuku   haha no ue ni to   inoru ko no
card ni miiri   mune atatakashi (haha no hi ni)

❀

Visiting my daughter's home
The spring flowers she picked for me scented the evening in lavender fair

訪づれし　娘の家づとの　春の花　うす紫に　匂ふ宵かな

Otozureshi   musume no iezuto no   haru no hana
usumurasaki ni   niou yoi kana

❀

Suffering with a toothache
I remember shedding tears on my mother's back
Listening to the drums as a lullaby

歯いたみに　泣きじゃくりつつ　母の背に　ききし大鼓の　子守歌はも

Haitami ni   nakijakuritsutsu   haha no se ni
kikishi taiko no   komoriuta wa mo

Chapter 6 – Children

It has been a long time since parents and sons dine together
Our sons' hair is thinning already

久方に　親子揃ひて　夕餉はむ　息子等の髪　はやうすうして

Hisakata ni　oyako soroite　yuge hamu
musukora no kami　haya usuushite

❀

As our sons dip in the bathtub
My thoughts hark back to my youth from their chatter I hear

久し振り　風呂につかりて　若き日を　思ひ出すらし　息子等の会話

Hisashiburi　furo ni tsukarite　wakaki hi o
omoidasurashi　musukora no kaiwa

Chapter Seven
Heaven, Earth, & Nature

I marvel at the line of giant waves along the seashore
Gallantly dashing waves flinging off, simple large sprays of nature's power

巨巌並び　波をけたてて　しぶきする　雄々しき様に　ただ魅せられぬ

Kyogan narabi　nami o ketatete　shibukisuru
ooshiki sama ni　tada miserarenu

❀

The appearence of the hills momentarily changes
Low over Manoa Valley a great rainbow marvels my eyes

マノア谷　刻々山の　相変り　大いなる虹に　まなこみはるも

Manoa dani　kokukoku yama no　so kawari
oinaru niji ni　manako miharumo

❀

The morning sun shining on the hillside
Rises beautifully before me as I sit at the breakfast table

朝の日に　かがやく山肌　美しく　目前に見て　朝げ食ぶるも

Asa no hi ni　kagayaku yamahada　utsukushiku
mokuzen ni mite　asage taburumo

Long ago passing through the kiawe woods[5]
I rode a horsedrawn buggy to an inn in Waikiki

その昔　キャベ林の　ワイキキを　馬車にゆられて　宿に行きしが

Sono mukashi   kiawe bayashi no   Waikiki o
basha ni yurarete   yado ni yukishiga

❀

Oh how extremely keen is the change here in Waikiki
To one who knows her past and present

今昔の　移り変りの　余りにも　はげしさ極む　ワイキキの地よ

Konjaku no   utsurikawari no   amari ni mo
hageshisa kiwamu   Waikiki no chi yo

❀

Up Kohala mountain we climb
While the wind and rain thrashes the highland below

コハラ山　のぼりてゆけば　ふもとなる　高原の雨あし　走りゆくみゆ

Kohala yama   noboriteyukeba   fumotonaru
kogen no ameashi   hashiriyuku miyu

---

[5] Mesquite

Chapter 7 – Heaven, Earth, & Nature

With the scent of fresh sea air
I reminisce of my younger days, clam digging and romping by the ocean

潮の香に　ふと思ひ出ぬ　若き日に　潮干狩して　興ぜし日日を

Shio no ka ni　futo omoidenu　wakaki hi ni
shiohigarishite　kyozeshi hibi o

❀

At the Gengetsu Bay, the maddened waves spray so fiercely
The power of nature numbs one's senses

荒波の　たけり狂へる　弦月湾　高くしぶきし　恐ろしき形相

Aranami no　takeri kurueru　Gengetsuwan
takaku shibukishi　osoroshiki gyoso

❀

Each clear morning I step out to the sidewalk
To see if the snow has capped the mountaintop

晴れし朝　舗道まで出で　山の雪　たしかむること　くせとはなりぬ

Hareshi asa　hodo made ide　yama no yuki
tashikamuru koto　kuse to wa narinu

After supper at the banks of the Wailoa river
I sit in ecstacy as the day closes silently over the heaven and earth

ワイロアの　川辺に夕餉　はみて後　暮れゆく天地の　静寂によふ

Wailoa no　kawabe ni yuge　hamite nochi
kureyuku tenchi no　seijaku ni you

❀

As all nature lies in slumber
Quietly the heavens twinkle like an ocean of stars

物みなは　眠りにおちて　大空は　静かにまばたく　星の海かも

Mono mina wa　nemuri ni ochite　ozora wa
shizukani mabataku　hoshi no umi ka mo

❀

We have climbed up to Pohakuloa
Where Kea[6] sleeps quietly in the white snow

ポハクロアに　のぼりてくれば　白雪の　ケアのねせまり　山気みちみち

Pohakuloa ni　noboritekureba　shirayuki no
Kea no ne semari　sanki michimichi

---

[6] Mauna Kea is a 13,796 foot mountain on the Big Island of Hawaii

From the heights swoops down the milky mist
And instantaneously enwraps me on the road

乳色の　霧のおりきて　忽ちに　我身をつつむ　高原の道

Chichiiro no　kiri no orikite　tachimachini
waga mi o tsutsumu　kogen no michi

❀

In the soft rain, I pick red plums
I am absorbed in nothingness, how refreshing it is!

小雨ついて　紅きプラムを　もぎゆけば　我なく他なく　心すがすがし

Kosame tsuite　akaki plum o　mogiyukeba
ware naku ta naku　kokoro sugasugashi

❀

Here and there mangoes hanging from the branches
This tells us summer has drawn near

おちこちに　マンゴの実の　なりさがる　姿に夏の　近きをぞ知る

Ochikochi ni　mango no mi no　narisagaru
sugata ni natsu no　chikaki o zo shiru

The papaya seed sent from Hilo has grown
And in Manoa bears sweet fruit too

ヒロの地より　送りしパパイヤの　種はえて　マノアの地にも　甘き実みのる

Hilo no chi yori　okurishi papaya no　tane haete
Manoa no chi ni mo　amaki mi minoru

❀

Papayas and bananas are ripe, hibiscus are also blooming
All are so dear to me

パパイヤも　バナナも熟し　なつかしき　ハイビスカスの　花も咲きおり

Papaya mo　banana mo jukushi　natsukashiki
hibiscus no　hana mo sakiori

❀

Every branch is bending with berries
What coloring, as if to herald that we're in autumn

ベリーの　総枝もたわわに　色づきぬ　秋にいりしと　告ぐる如くに

Berry no　soshi mo tawawani　irozukinu
aki ni irishi to　tsuguru gotokuni

The withered leaves of 'ulu (bread fruit) flutter in the evening breeze
And down on the ground draw autumn patterns

夕風に　ウルのわくら葉　はらはらと　土の上にえがく　秋の模様を

Yukaze ni   ulu (bread fruit) no wakuraba   harahara to
tsuchi no ue ni egaku   aki no moyo o

❀

Oh, the night view from a hill of San Francisco City
I hold my breath at the ocean of flaming lights

桑港の　丘より眺めし　夜の街　火の大海に　はつと息のむ

Soko no   oka yori nagameshi   yoru no machi
hi no taikai ni   hatto iki nomu

❀

San Francisco lives in time-honored tradition
The style of houses and the outlook of the town

桑港は　古き伝統に　生きてをり　家の姿も　町のたたずまひも

Soko wa   furuki dento ni   ikiteori
ie no sugata mo   machi no tatazumai mo

Nature's art is so skillful
Standing upright into the clouds are the rocky peaks of Yosemite

大自然の　技巧たくみに　ヨセミテの　岩の峯峯　雲つきてたつ

Daishizen no　giko-takumini　Yosemite no
iwa no minemine　kumotsukite tatsu

Chapter 7 – Heaven, Earth, & Nature

Chapter Eight
Life

Through all these years
No songs I sang, no poems did I compose, but in silence life has passed

此の年月　歌も歌はず　詩も詠まず　ただ黙々と　生きて来しかも

Kono toshitsuki　uta mo utawazu　shi mo yomazu
tada mokumokuto　ikitekishikamo

❁

A swarm of dragonflies danced gaily by
Comforting me this clear autumn afternoon

とんぼの群　たのしく舞ひて　病む我を　なぐさめゆきぬ　秋晴れの午後

Tonbo no mure　tanoshiku maite　yamu ware o
nagusameyukinu　akibare no gogo

❁

As I lay in my sickbed
I perceive the blessings of the long years and months
I happily spent in sound health

病床にて　長き年月　健かに　たのしく過せし　めぐみを思ふ

Byosho ni te　nagaki nengetsu　sukoyakani
tanoshiku sugoseshi　megumi o omou

Nothing is comparable to having the pleasure of being blessed
With the thrill and joy of full recovery

すこやかに　なりにし幸の　喜は　譬ふるものさへ　あらぬ感激

Sukoyakani　narinishi sachi no　yorokobi wa
tatouru mono sae　aranu kangeki

❀

I hope for a useful way to spend my years
My heart is full to the brim with content

有効に　余生を送る　すべを知り　みちたりし心　得たしと思ふ

Yukoni　yosei o okuru　sube o shiri
michitarishi kokoro　etashi to omou

❀

From Tokyo my niece has come
What a joy to talk with her after so many years

東都より　来りし姪と　久々に　なつかしみあひて　語る喜び

Toto yori　kitarishi mei to　hisabisani
natsukashimiaite　kataru yorokobi

Half a century has passed already in this land
Yet there is a feeling that something is still missing

半世紀　はや過ぎ去りぬ　此の地にて　何か足りなき　もののあるまま

Hanseiki　haya sugisarinu　kono chi ni te
nani ka tarinaki　mono no arumama

❁

More than fifty years have passed
As a housewife and yet how ignorant have I lived

妻の座に　五十余年も　ありてなほ　みやびも知らず　愚鈍に生くるも

Tsuma no za ni　gojuyonen mo　arite nao
miyabi mo shirazu　gudon ni ikurumo

❁

I feel I have done my duty
Now I happily compose poems as the night passes

我がつとめ　はたし終えたる　心地して　夜はたのしも　詩作に更けゆく

Waga tsutome　hatashioetaru　kokochishite
yoru wa tanoshimo　shisaku ni fukeyuku

So many years I have lived
With the aid of a magnifying glass and dictionary

幾とせを　拡大鏡と　辞典とに　ささえられつつ　生きてきしかも

Ikutose o   kakudaikyo to   jiten to ni
sasaeraretsutsu   ikitekishi kamo

❀

In my treasured thoughts - far and near, past and present
You may wander freely as you please

思索する　ことはたのしも　無償にて　遠近古今　おもむくがまま

Shisakusuru   koto wa tanoshimo   mushonite
enkin kokon   omomuku ga mama

❀

When young,
I was a champion at karuta[7] cards in which I took great pride
But alas, I can hardly remember people's names as I grow old

若き日には　かるたの選手を　誇りしが　老いては人の　名さえ忘れつ

Wakaki hi ni wa   karuta no senshu o   hokorishi ga
oite wa hito no   na sae wasuretsu

---

[7] Poetry playing cards

Deep anger burning in my heart
With restraint I calmly write the answer

心底に　もゆる怒を　おさえつつ　ただおだやかに　返りごとかく

Shinsoko ni　moyuru ikari o　osaetsutsu
tada odayakani　kaerigoto kaku

❀

I recall as I cook beans in my kitchen
In my youth, making sweetbean rice cake with my mother

くりや辺に　豆たきおれば　若き日に　母と作りし　おはぎ思ひ出ず

Kuriyabe ni　mame takioreba　wakaki hi ni
haha to tsukurishi　ohagi omoiizu

❀

In ancient days a love affair was merely a scene of daily routine
So I perceive through the old Manyo shu poems[8]

いにしえは　恋ものどけく　なりはひの　一こまなりしと　万葉歌にしる

Inishie wa　koi mo nodokeku　nariwai no
hitokomanarishi to　Manyoka ni shiru

---

[8] Oldest recorded Japanese poetry from approximately 400-750 AD

With my advancing age
My morning exercises become more zealous and longer

年とれば　とる程朝の　健康法　熱入り来り　長時間となる

Toshitoreba　toruhodo asa no　kenkoho
netsu irikitari　chojikan to naru

My heart warms at the thought of my sister waiting for me
At the extreme shore of this ocean

此の海の　極まる岸に　待ちわびる　妹のあれば　心あたたかし

Kono umi no　kiwamaru kishi ni　machiwabiru
imoto no areba　kokoro atatakashi

My sister writes in her letter of decorating Mother's grave,
On Higan Day[9], with chrysanthemums from both of us

彼岸には　母のみ墓に　二人分　菊かざりしと　妹はたよりす

Higan ni wa　haha no mihaka ni　futaribun
kiku kazarishi to　imoto wa tayorisu

---

[9] Buddhist's traditional time for visiting cemeteries; falls on the the Vernal and Autumnal Equinox

Hanging the charity pan they clang the bell
And to the sound people pass to and fro in hurrying steps

慈善鍋　かけてうちふる　鈴の音に　ゆきかふ人の　足どりせわし

Jizennabe　kakete uchifuru　suzu no ne ni
yukikau hito no　ashidori sewashi

❀

On New Year Day, as I contemplate on poems,
I vaguely long for the odor of Chinese ink

新春に　歌思ふとき　何となく　墨の香りの　恋しくなりぬ

Shinshun ni　uta omou toki　nantonaku
sumi no kaori no　koishikunarinu

❀

As I pass my 77 years of joyous longevity
As I reflect on what the Divine Grace bestowed upon me all these days
To my lips rise a hymn of praise

喜寿の年の　峠にたちて　こしかたの　めぐみを思ひ　讃歌出づるも

Kiju no toshi no　toge ni tachite　koshikata no
megumi o omoi　sanka izurumo

At the mountain hotel I appreciate the rich furnishing in Indian design
What an agreeable traditional harmony

山の宿　古調豊かに　調度など　インディアンのデザイン　みちてたのしき

Yama no yado   kocho yutakani   chodo nado
Indian no design   michite tanoshiki

❀

Burning bundles of old letters, to and fro, in my heart rises
Images after images of my dear friends

文がらの　束を焼きつつ　なつかしき　おもかげあまた　胸にゆきかふ

Fumigara no   taba o yakitsutsu   natsukashiki
omokage amata   mune ni yukikau

❀

On the elder's forehead are wrinkles,
That shine in glory these days

老人（おいびと）の　ひたひのしわの　各々に　栄光かがやく　此の日此の頃

Oibito no   hitai no shiwa no   onoono ni
eiko kagayaku   kono hi kono goro

If Mother were here, a centenarian she would be
Surviving four chronological eras[10]

母いませば　百の齢とは　なりまさん　四代の年号　生きぬきしものを

Haha imaseba　hyaku no toshi to wa　narimasan
yodai no nengo　ikinukishi mono o

❀

This diagnosis of the paralysis of my throat
At this stage of old age, it does not tug the heartstring of anyone

咽喉の麻痺　との診断　我が胸に　するどくひびく　老いの身にして

Nodo no mahi　to no shindan　waga mune ni
surudoku hibiku　oi no mi ni shite

❀

Many months have passed, since I lost my voice,
I fill a whole notebook of my conversation

声なき日々　はや幾月か　すぎ去りて　筆談の帳も　一冊終りぬ

Koe naki hibi　haya ikutsuki ka　sugisarite
hitsudan no cho mo　issatsu owarinu

---

[10] Reign era of Japanese emperor's Meiji, Taisho, Showa, and Heisei

Mother gently taught me in the tea ceremony
In my heart I sobbed, as a child so young

茶室にて　母はやさしく　教えしを　幼きわれは　心になきぬ

Chashitsu ni te　haha wa yasashiku　oshieshi o
osanaki ware wa　kokoro ni nakinu

❀

Strolling in the evening, along the banks of cherry blossom trees
Grandma recited Shunmin's poem[11] for me, how I long for her!

夜桜の　つつみゆきつつ　春眠の　詩を教へられし　祖母のなつかし

Yozakura no　tsutsumi yukitsutsu　shunmin no
shi o oshierareshi　sobo no natsukashi

❀

The winds rages down from the mountains
Night in Manoa is eerie indeed as the house shakes in the wind[12]

山颪し　はげしく吹きて　家きしむ　マノアの夜は　無気味なるかも

Yamaoroshi　hageshiku fukite　ie kishimu
Manoa no yoru wa　bukiminaru kamo

---

[11] (Shunmin) Meng Haoran - Chinese poet 681-740AD
[12] Calm tradewinds by day are replaced by high winds from the mountains at night

Chapter 8 – Life

Shut in the valley of Manoa in the storm
I long for the lovely sky of Hilo

マノア谷の　嵐の中に　こもり居て　好天のヒロを　恋しく思えり

Manoa tani no　arashi no naka ni　komoriite
koten no Hilo o　koishiku omoeri

❁

Though advancing in age, once my mind is set on poetry
Joy whirls around and my heart is filled with sunshine

老ひぬれど　歌思ふ時　喜びの　うずまき来り　心かがやく

Oinuredo　uta omou toki　yorokobi no
uzumaki kitari　kokoro kagayaku

❁

A tune from songs I learned from my grandfather
Flows from my my lips, can it be "Viewing Scarlet Maples?"

祖父君に　習ひしうたひの　一節が　口つきて出づ　紅葉狩かも

Sofugimi ni　naraishi utai no　hitofushi ga
kuchi tsukiteizu　momijigari kamo

Chapter Nine
Odds and Ends

Chapter 9 – Odds and Ends

As I bid farewell to you, I crossed the sea to these southern islands
Where no sleet falls or plum blossoms scent

海越えて　君と別れて　来し島は　みぞれもふらず　梅も匂わず

Umi koete　kimi to wakarete　koshi shima wa
mizore mo furazu　ume mo niowazu

❀

My dear one sits by the window where the white plum grows
Playing on the piano the songs of spring

君は今　かの白梅の　窓辺にて　ピアノに春の　うたをひくかも

Kimi wa ima　kano shiraume no　madobe ni te
piano ni haru no　uta o hikukamo

❀

If the wind blows, I pine for my hometown
If it rains, I long for my sister, these days of winter

風吹けば　都恋しく　雨ふれば　妹思ふ　冬のこの頃

Kaze fukeba　miyako koishiku　ame fureba
imoto omou　fuyu no konogoro

I cannot speak the sadness of the past or hide it
Alas 'tis the path I have followed

語らんに　余りに悲し　つつまんに　心もだゆる　歩みきし道

Kataran ni   amari ni kanashi   tsutsuman ni
kokoro modayuru   ayumikishi michi

❀

The second month of the lunar calendar, to the park I stroll
And on the lawn I bathe in the morning sun
What joy beneath this February sky

公園の　芝生にゆきて　朝の日に　ひたるもうれし　きさらぎの空

Koen no   shibafu ni yukite   asa no hi ni
hitaru mo ureshi   kisaragi no sora

❀

At the end of a majestic line of leaves
Like red lips parted the orchid blooms

いかめしき　葉のつらなりの　その先に　赤き唇　開くかに蘭

Ikameshiki   ha no tsuranari no   sono saki ni
akaki kuchibiru   hiraku kaniran

Chapter 9 – Odds and Ends

I yearn for the summer night display
The early fresh greens and field flowers blooming on the Musashino plain

恋しきは　夏の夜店と　新緑に　草の花さく　武蔵野の原

Koishiki wa　natsu no yomise to　shinryoku ni
kusa no hana saku　Musashino no hara

❀

The evening of this southern land
Their sad stories are sung by the natives[13] to the strum of guitars

南国の夜　物語りは　悲しけれ　土人の歌と　ギターのひびきと

Nangoku no yoru　monogatari wa　kanashikere
dojin no uta to　guitar no hibiki to

❀

I love the night as it deepens over the park
In the shadows of solitude there's the murmur of the tripping waves

公園の　夜更けはうれし　寂寞の　やみにさざめく　波の音あり

Koen no　yofuke wa ureshi　sekibaku no
yami ni sazameku　nami no oto ari

---

[13] Hawaiians

The snow-capped mountain appeared brightly in the clear sky
Joy springs at such a seldom sight

雪山の　あかるく空に　出たるも　たまさかなれば　喜びのわく

Yukiyama no　akaruku sora ni　idetaru mo
tamasakanareba　yorokobi no waku

❀

How lovely the mountain in purplish shade
More so is its snow white crown

山の色　紫なるも　うれしきが　雪のかむりは　更に好まし

Yama no iro　murasakinaru mo　ureshiki ga
yuki no kamuri wa　sarani konomashi

❀

Born in a town in great Edo[14]
Memories are dear as I look into the past

大江戸の　町に生れし　我なりし　思出追へば　なつかしきかな

Oedo no　machi ni umareshi　ware narishi
omoide oeba　natsukashikikana

---

[14] Tokyo

A young girl, my friend, working in a thread and yarn shop
Such bright eyes had she with both corners tinted with rouge

つぶら眼の　目ぢりに細く　紅させし　糸屋の娘　我友なりき

Tsubura me no　meijiri ni hosoku　beni saseshi
itoya no museme　waga tomo nariki

❀

She was a maid, so becoming with hair dressed in peach colored ribbons
A dappled ribbon tied loosely at the momoware[15]

桃われに　桃色かのこを　ふくませし　髪の似合ひし　少女なりしが

Momoware ni　momoiro kanoko o　fukumaseshi
kami no niaishi　shojo narishiga

❀

There was a large gingko tree beside Benten Mountain
I remember my kimono sleeves getting heavier
With the gingko-nuts I gathered

浅草の　弁天山の　大いちょう　ぎんなんひろう　袖重かりき

Asakusa no　Bentenyama no　daiicho
ginnan hirou　sode omokariki

---

[15] A hair style – in this case, a style for young unmarried ladies

When spring is here my thoughts are seized with longings
For the Ueno art exhibition[16]
Of Bunten paintings and other memories I miss so deeply

春来れば　上野にありし　文展の　絵など思ひ　恋しくなりぬ

Haru kureba　Ueno ni arishi　Bunten no
e nado omoi　koishiku narinu

❀

I was lost in ecstacy in a dream listening to the (great) actress Sumako
Reciting her lines that evening in early spring at the Imperial Theatre

帝劇の　すま子の声に　よわされし　夢のようなる　初春の宵

Teigeki no　Sumako no koe ni　yowasareshi
Yume no yonaru　hatsuharu no yoi

❀

I shudder to hear of the earthquake
That shook the capital city[17] in midday so violently this early fall

初秋の　まひるに大地　ゆり動く　都のたより　きいておののく

Hatsuaki no　mahiru ni daichi　yuriugoku
miyako no tayori　kikite ononoku

---

[16] Cultural mueseum in Tokyo
[17] Tokyo

Chapter 9 – Odds and Ends

If the earth shakes, flames would sweep up,
And what waits man is but death destined

地ふるえば　炎も上り　地もさけて　死の運命のみ　人を待ちけり

Chi furueba   honoo mo agari   chi mo sakete
shi no unmei nomi   hito o machikeri

❀

Mother, friends, beloved teachers, and my brothers and sisters
How are they faring? Violently my heart throbs in worry

母上は　友はおん師は　はらからは　如何におわすと　胸のとどろく

Hahaue wa   tomo wa onshi wa   harakara wa
ikani owasu to   mune no todoroku

❀

On evenings I fear my dreams
With a deep sigh I pass another day

夢などを　うらないて見る　宵などは　太息をつきて　今日も暮しぬ

Yume nado o   uranaitemiru   yoi nado wa
futoiki o tsukite   kyo mo kurashinu

I wait in sadness longing to hear
And twenty days have passed in vain

待ちわびる　悲しき願ひの　いつまでか　つづきつづきて　二十日もすぎぬ

Machiwabiru　kanashiki negai no　itsu made ka
tsuzuki tsuzukite　hatsuka mo suginu

❀

High or low, rich or poor,
Prostrate before the power unseen

貴きも　いやしきものも　貧も富も　みえぬ力に　ただひれふしぬ

Totoki mo　iyashiki mono mo　hin mo fu mo
mienu chikara ni　tada hirefushinu

❀

The calls of the frantic woman and the child for its mother's breast
So pitiful are their voices

子をよびて　狂える女　母よびて　乳をたずぬる　子の声悲し

Ko o yobite　kurueru onna　haha yobite
chichi o tazunuru　ko no koe kanashi

Chapter 9 – Odds and Ends

Are they alive or dead, wounded or ill
Over and over I imagine their fate

生か死か　傷のいたみか　病ひかと　よしなし言を　くりかえし見る

Sei ka shi ka　kizu no itami ka　yamai ka to
yoshinashigoto o　kurikaeshimiru

Chapter Ten
Elegy

Chapter 10 — Elegy

The snowcapped mountain
Refreshes my inner thirst and stimulates my heart
With thoughts and hopes these monotonous days

もの多く　思はするかな　雪山は　刺激なき日の　かわける胸に

Mono ooku　omowasurukana　yukiyama wa
shigeki naki hi no　kawakeru mune ni

❀

In my youth I dreamt of a lifetime
Writing poems to my heart's content

一生を　よみて歌ひて　終らんと　思ひし事も　若き日にあり

Issho o　yomite utaite　owaranto
omoishi koto mo　wakaki hi ni ari

❀

On days when the silvery delicate rain falls
My mind overflows with poems

しろがねの　細雨ふる日は　かがやける　心起りて　歌思ふかな

Shirogane no　saiu furu hi wa　kagayakeru
kokoro okorite　uta omoukana

Softly shines the sun in the tropical fall rain
Over the garden this morning where the sun lits faintly

うす日さす　朝の庭面に　ふる雨の　細く光れる　南国の秋

Usubi sasu   asa no niwamo ni   furu ame no
hosoku hikareru   nangoku no aki

❀

I gaze at the six chicks morning and evening
What strength and beauty of life they show

朝な夕な　六つのひなの　育ちゆく　生の姿の　強く美し

Asa na yu na   muttsu no hina no   sodachiyuku
sei no sugata no   tsuyoku utsukushi

❀

What an amusing sight to watch the chicks like cotton balls
Feeding in excited happiness

わたまりの　ようなるひなの　喜びて　餌をはむ姿　愛らしきかな

Watamari no   yonaru hina no   yorokobite
e o hamu sugata   airashikikana

The winter sun sets fast, valuing the last light, the bird cries
An oshiroi[18] flower blooms close by

冬深き　日あしを惜しみ　なく鳥の　そのかたえなる　おしろいの花

Fuyu fukaki　hiashi o oshimi　naku tori no
sono kataenaru　oshiroi no hana

❀

In the evening glow I listen to the mourning of the sea
Like a corpse leaning against the coconut tree

夕ぐれの　海のなげきに　きき入りぬ　むくろの如く　やしにもたれて

Yugure no　umi no nageki ni　kikiirinu
mukuro no gotoku　yashi ni motarete

❀

I have become a mother
I adore my child's cheerful heart beaming bright in happiness

赤々と　明るき色に　生きる子の　心羨やむ　母とはなりぬ

Akaakato　akaruki iro ni　ikiru ko no
kokoro urayamu　haha to wa narinu

---

[18] Mirabilis – clavillia or beauty of the night

My mother, after raising five children
Getting old, she is very content

いとけなき　五つの命　守りつつ　老ひゆく母の　心たのしも

Itokenaki   itsutsu no inochi   mamoritsutsu
oiyuku haha no   kokoro tanoshimo

❀

We took the beloved word Kyo[19]
For our daughter's name, she's now three, the darling dear

なつかしき　京の一字を　名にとりし　我子愛らし　年三つにして

Natsukashiki   Kyo no ichiji o   na ni torishi
waga ko airashi   toshi mittsu ni shite

❀

I look into my sick child's face
Tears fill my eyes at the hospital this afternoon as the thin rain is falling

病める子の　顔をのぞきて　涙しぬ　細き雨ふる　病院の午後

Yameru ko no   kao o nozokite   namidashinu
hosoki ame furu   byoin no gogo

---

[19] As in Tokyo – my birthplace

I call her name and kiss her then she smiles
I press my cheek against her cheek and she giggles with delight

名をよびて　口づけすれば　ほほえみぬ　頬ずりすれば　声たてて笑ふ

Na o yobite　kuchizukesureba　hohoeminu
hohozurisureba　koe tatete warau

❀

On my deceased child's grave a song is carved
As I begin to sing it, my grief deepens more

死にし子の　墓にしるせし　歌などを　うたえば更に　悲しみのわく

Shinishi ko no　haka ni shiruseshi　uta nado o
utaeba sarani　kanashimi no waku

❀

From the seeds of the flowers I offered to her grave
My child rests in peace in a flower garden

子の墓に　手むけし花の　種こぼれ　花畑の中に　子はねむりおり

Ko no haka ni　tamukeshi hana no　tane kobore
hanabatake no naka ni　ko wa nemuriori

On a clear day I feel relaxed
On a rainy day I feel peaceful, so sweet is this mountain villa

晴れし日も　心よけれど　雨の日も　心なごみて　たのし山荘

Hareshi hi mo　kokoroyokeredo　ame no hi mo
kokoro nagomite　tanoshi sanso

❀

In the tender rain, red plums I keep picking
Then you nor I exist, how refreshed my heart is

小雨ついて　紅きプラムを　もぎゆけば　我なく他なく　心すがすがし

Kosame tsuite　akaki plum o　mogiyukeba
ware naku hoka naku　kokoro sugasugashi

❀

At the mountain villa we sit surrounding the cauldron
I pick up my chopsticks, the mountain air stimulates my appetite

山荘に　鍋をかこみて　はしとれば　山の気みちて　そそる食慾

Sanso ni　nabe o kakomite　hashi toreba
yama no ki michite　sosoru shokuyoku

Chapter 10 – Elegy

Out into the world we'll go and someday justify your parental love
Till then, keep in good health so our children tell us

世にいでて　親にむくゆる　それまでは　健やかなれと　語る我子ら

Yo ni idete　oya ni mukuyuru　sore made wa
sukoyakanare to　kataru waga kora

❀

We talk over our children's future
Thus our silver wedding day we quietly spend together

我子らの　行末などを　語らひて　銀婚の日を　静かに過す

Wagakora no　yukusue nado o　kataraite
ginkon no hi o　shizukani sugosu

❀

Many dreams of my heart I explore
I enjoy myself these recent years

さまざまの　心の夢を　のばしては　一人たのしむ　この幾年を

Samazama no　kokoro no yume o　nobashite wa
hitori tanoshimu　kono ikutoshi o

May this child grow up to give true service to this world and people
Thus I the mother prays

世に人に　まことの奉仕　いたす子と　ならまほしとぞ　祈るこの母

Yo ni hito ni　makoto no hoshi　itasu ko to
naramahoshi to zo　inoru kono haha

❀

Spring is here, the white lilies are in full bloom
Even Soloman in all his glory cannot outshine these lilies white

ソロモンの　栄華にまさる　白百合の　みごとにさき出ずる　春とはなりぬ

Solomon no　eiga ni masaru　shirayuri no
migotoni sakiizuru　haru to wa narinu

❀

Again today
I devote myself to strengthen my wish to live in love and righteousness

今日も又　愛のみわざを　はげみつつ　正しく生きる　願ひは強し

Kyo mo mata　ai no miwaza o　hagemi tsutsu
tadashiku ikiru　negai wa tsuyoshi

Chapter 10 – Elegy

**When I think of the Divine God that has guided me since childhood
The deepness and sacredness touch me**

幼きより　導きたまひし　みめぐみを　思えばふかく　たえに貴し

*Osanaki yori　michibikitamaishi　mimegumi o
omoeba fukaku　tae ni totoshi*

❀

**Behold the birds in the sky, the lilies in the field
These words of Jesus sound strong and sacred to me**

空の鳥　野の百合思えと　のたまひし　イエスのみ言葉　強く貴し

*Sora no tori　no no yuri omoe to　notamaishi
Iesu no mikotoba　tsuyoku totoshi*

❀

**Once we happen to meet our gaze to the other's hair
And exchange smiles, a habit formed since when?**

たまさかに　会へば互ひの　髪を見て　ほほえむくせの　いつよりかつきし

*Tamasakani　aeba tagai no　kami o mite
hohoemu kuse no　itsu yori ka tsukishi*

This evening as I go to bed
Hoping I may bid the last farewell with a smile

永別の　時には笑みて　ゆかましと　願ひて今宵　ふしどには入る

Eibetsu no　toki ni wa emite　yukamashi to
negaite koyoi　fushido ni hairu

❀

On Mother's Day I was chosen "Mother of the Year"
And with joy I received a beautiful floral bouquet

母の日に　今年の母と　えらばれて　美しき花たば　受くる感激

Haha no hi ni　kotoshi no haha to　erabarete
Utsukushiki hanataba　ukuru kangeki

❀

In tears of happiness I pray
May my body and soul be purified making me into your useful instrument

感激の　涙の中に　身もたまも　きよめ用ひて　給えと祈る

Kangeki no　namida no naka ni　mi mo tama mo
kiyome mochiite　tamae to inoru

At this old age I become ill and receive God's warmth
And I feel more deeply his neverending love

老ひて病む　神の警告　身にうけて　深きみ心　しみじみ思ふ

Oite yamu   kami no keikoku   mi ni ukete
fukaki mikokoro   shimijimi omou

❀

Sick in bed feeling lonely
My heart is touched by my friend's surprise visit

病みおれば　心淋しく　訪づれし　友のまごころ　心にしみる

Yamioreba   kokoro sabishiku   otozureshi
tomo no magokoro   kokoro ni shimiru

❀

Chrysanthemums have appeared in the shops
They remind me of fall in my hometown

ふるさとの　秋思はする　菊の花　店頭に見る　頃とはなりぬ

Furusato no   aki omowasuru   kiku no hana
tento ni miru   koro to wa narinu

When I hear of Mauna Kea lovely with snow
I long for the sky of my hometown

マウナケヤに　白雪つもり　美しと　ききてなつかし　ふるさとの空

Mauna Kea ni　shirayuki tsumori　uruwashi to
kikite natsukashi　furusato no sora

❀

My friends send me recovery notes with prayers
My eyes blur with tears for their affection

いえよとの　祈をこめし　寄せ書の　友の情に　ただ涙しぬ

Ieyo to no　inori o komeshi　yosegaki no
tomo no nasake ni　tada namida shinu

❀

A friend in Atami wrote to me
She learned of my illness when she read the poetry column from Hawaii

ハワイよりの　紙上の歌に　我病むを　知りしと熱海の　友はたよりす

Hawaii yori no　shijo no uta ni　ware yamu o
shirishi to Atami no　tomo wa tayorisu

Snugly at home in the valley listening to the wind from the mountain
Writing poetry is pleasing indeed

谷間ひの　家にこもりて　山風の　音をききつつ　歌よむはよし

Taniai no　ie ni komorite　yamakaze no
oto o kikitsutsu　uta yomu wa yoshi

❀

My beloved friends pass away one after another
Loneliness presses upon my heart

なつかしき　友次々と　逝きまして　淋しさ胸に　せまり来るかも

Natsukashiki　tomo tsugitsugito　yukimashite
sabishisa mune ni　semarikurukamo

❀

Most of our many friends have left this world
We happily marvel to have lived to this day

他界せし　友多き中に　我らよく　生き残りしを　喜び合へり

Takaiseshi　tomo ooki naka ni　warera yoku
ikinokorishi o　yorokobiaeri

All these years we were so attached in friendship
Yet she has passed away leaving me in loneliness

長き年　親しみあいし　友ゆきて　淋しさ胸に　せまり来るかも

Nagaki toshi   shitashimiaishi   tomo yukite
sabishisa mune ni   semarikuru kamo

Chapter Eleven
The Trip

Chapter 11 – The Trip

Various numbers of "tanka" were found in one of Kurenai's notebooks. It contained poems remembering the trip in Izu Peninsula with a group of close friends. How Kurenai enjoyed talks of the good old days with her dear friends. The trips to Hakone and Atami also must have been quite impressive to her.

This visit to her motherland was full of unforgetable memories, and there should be more of such poems still. However it was quite a task to collect the poems, which would not have been possible without Yoshimi san's kind concern and assistance.

❁

**With my classmates I took a trip around the Izu Peninsula
What a happy group of six we were!**

同級の　友どち六たり　共々に　伊豆をめぐりぬ　たのしなつかし

*Dokyu no　tomodochi rokutari　tomodomo ni
Izu o megurinu　tanoshi natsukashi*

❁

**Every morning I enjoy the hot spring bath
The visit to Japan was worthwhile after all**

朝々に　温泉に入る　快さ　日本に来りし　甲斐ありと思ふ

*Asaasa ni　onsen ni iru　kokoroyosa
Nihon ni kitarishi　kai ari to omou*

Our inn surrounded by mountains, it is a hot spring village
The winter day is as warm as that of spring

我宿は　山にかこまれし　温泉郷　冬日も春の　如くあたたか

Waga yado wa　yama ni kakomareshi　onsenkyo
fuyubi mo haru no　gotoku atataka

❁

In Minami (southern) Izu
You will see many hothouses using the hot spring

温泉を　利用して立つ　温室の　数多くあり　南伊豆の地

Onsen o　riyoshite tatsu　onshitsu no
kazu ooku ari　Minami Izu no chi

❁

Tulips, white lillies, azaleas, and many other flowers
In the midwinter bloom in the hothouse

チューリップ　白百合つつじ　数々の　花咲きほこる　真冬の温室

Tulip　shirayuri tsutsuji　kazukazu no
hana sakihokoru　mafuyu no onshitsu

In the hothouse I see lots of dark blue eggplants
And blue pepper also shining brightly grow

紺色の　茄子あまた見ゆ　温室に　ブルーペパーなど　つややかにみのる

Koniro no　nasu amata miyu　onshitsu ni
blue pepper nado　tsuyayakani minoru

❁

In South Izu the pea flowers blossom
The oranges are gay in color too

南伊豆　えんどうの花　盛りなり　みかんの色も　鮮やかにして

Minami Izu　endo no hana　sakarinari
mikan no iro mo　azayakani shite

❁

In the Southern Izu Peninsula
'Tis midwinter and white plum blossoms everywhere you see

伊豆半島　南にくれば　寒入りと　いうに白梅　あまた咲きおり

Izu Hanto　minami ni kureba　kaniri to
iu ni shiraume　amata sakiori

Irozaki at the south end of the peninsula
Giant rocks are standing in line out in the sea, how beautiful it is

半島の　南のはしの　石廊崎　奇岩並びて　海美しき

Hanto no　minami no hashi no　Irozaki
kigan narabite　umi utsukushiki

❀

They say that Shimoda had been an open country land
No wonder there are so many historical remains

其の昔　開国の地と　なりしといふ　下田の地には　史績多かり

Sono mukashi　kaikoku no chi to　narishi to iu
Shimoda no chi ni wa　shiseki ookari

❀

Carved on the monument is a passage from Harris'[20] diary
Having a bad night of being attacked by swarming mosquitos

ハリスの碑に　ほりし日記の　一節に　おそひ来る蚊に　ねむられずとあり

Harris no hi ni　horishi nikki no　issetsu ni
osoikuru ka ni　nemurarezu to ari

---

[20] A Christian merchant who lived in Shimoda and was one of the founders of the Society for the Prevention of Cruelty to Animals; he later became First Consul General to Japan 1856

There are many beautiful sights in Shimoda
Oura, Wakaura, Kakizaki and others

下田には　美しき地の　あまたあり　大浦和歌浦　姉崎などと

Shimoda ni wa　utsukushiki chi no　amata ari
Oura Wakaura　Kakizaki nado to

❀

We ascended the Akane hill of Oura
Where the seven islands of Izu are viewed in one sight

大浦の　赤根の丘に　のぼり来れば　伊豆の七島　一望に見ゆ

Oura no　Akane no oka ni　noborikureba
Izu no shichito　ichibo ni miyu

❀

In the garden of the shrine stands high the statue of Shoin
Overlooking the port of Shimoda

下田港を　見下す如く　松陰の　像そそり立つ　社の庭に

Shimodako o　miorosugotoku　Shoin no
zo sosoritatsu　yashiro no niwa ni

I come with my friends to Goura Hakone
At this mountain villa in the misty rain my heart is filled with emotion

雨けぶる　箱根強羅の　山荘に　友だちと来て　楽しさ極む

Ame keburu　Hakone Gora no　sanso ni
tomodachi to kite　tanoshisa kiwamu

❁

At the hot spring bath, we wash each other's back
The memories of our young days come back to us

温泉にて　互ひに背中　流しあひ　若き日の思出　よみがえり来る

Onsen ni te　tagai ni senaka　nagashiai
wakaki hi no omoide　yomigaerikuru

❁

We circle around the table and talk about the memories
Of bygone dormitory life days, it's a happy sweet moment

テーブルを　かこみて語る　寄宿舎の　昔語りも　なつかしうれし

Table o　kakomite kataru　kishukusha no
mukashigatari mo　natsukashi ureshi

It seems like only yesterday, to hear my friend speak
Of the fifty year old stories of the past

五十年の　昔語りとは　思はれず　昨日の如く　友は語れる

Gojunen no　mukashigatari to wa　omowarezu
kino no gotoku　tomo wa katareru

✿

Step by step, in straw woven sandals, up the pass we climbed
Now in a flash the cable car takes us

わらじふみ　のぼりし峠も　ケーブルの　車にのれば　つかのまにゆく

Waraji fumi　noborishi toge mo　cable no
kuruma ni noreba　tsukanoma ni yuku

✿

The hilltop famed for its Jukkoku[21] view
We reach and there stands Mt Fuji in white, so beautiful

十国の　ながめのあると　いう丘に　のぼれば真白き　富士の美し

Jukkoku no　nagame no aru to　iu oka ni
noboreba mashiroki　Fuji no uruwashi

---

[21] Ten countries (literal translation) – grand vista

Similar to Taikan's[22] vignette drawings, an extreme type of art
So is this view of the misty mountains far beyond

大観の　絵の如もやに　ぼかされし　遠き山々　美の極みかも

Taikan no　e no goto moya ni　bokasareshi
toki yamayama　bi no kiwami ka mo

⚘

Joining a Christian tourist party
As if in a dream I enjoy the trip

キリスト教　観光団に　加はりて　夢見る如き　旅をたのしむ

Kirisutokyo　kankodan ni　kuwawarite
yumemiru gotoki　tabi o tanoshimu

⚘

The party also visits my hometown
Nakamise Street and Kannondo[23]

団員も　我がふる里を　見給えり　仲見世通り　観音堂も

Danin mo　waga furusato o　mitamaeri
Nakamise doori　Kannondo mo

---

[22] Yokoyama Taikan – foremost scenery artist
[23] Famous Buddhist temple

My heart is delighted to see
Dear Asakusa Town and Kannondo, also the Nitenmom Gate

我心　なつかしみたり　浅草を　観音堂や　二天門をも

Waga kokoro　natsukashimitari　Asakusa o
Kannondo ya　Nitenmon o mo

❀

I stroll along Shonan Beach
And find myself reciting quietly Psalm Nineteen

湘南の　海辺をゆけば　おのづから　詩篇十九を　くちずさみをり

Shonan no　umibe o yukeba　onozukara
Shihen juku o　kuchizusamiori

❀

Along the Hakone Highway we go
No view in the thick fog, the only sound is the girl guide's voice

霧深き　箱根路ゆけば　視野もなく　ガイド娘の　声のみひびく

Kiki fukaki　Hakoneji yukeba　shiya mo naku
guide musume no　koe nomi hibiku

When Lake Ashi comes in view
The fog clears up revealing the red torii of Gongendo

芦の湖の　ひらけるあたり　霧もはれ　権現堂の　鳥居もあかし

Ashinoko no　hirakeru atari　kiri mo hare
Gongendo no　torii mo akashi

❁

My dream came true today
As I'm happily walking and approaching the Ise Shrine

いつの日か　来らん望　かなへられ　伊勢参道を　歩む喜び

Itsu no hi ka　kitaran nozomi　kanaerare
Ise Sando o　ayumu yorokobi

❁

Gazing up and down the trees which soar skyward in rows
In silence I approach this walk

そびえ立つ　並木を見上げ　見下ろしつ　只黙々と　参道をゆく

Sobietatsu　namiki o miage　mioroshitsu
tada mokumokuto　sando o yuku

The surface of the rice field ripples like waves
How lovely it is at harvest time

豊なる　みのりの田の面　穂波たち　とり入れ近く　美しきかな

Yutakanaru　minori no ta no mo　honami tachi
toriire chikaku　utsukushikikana

❀

Seto Inland Sea is like a garden
Inokuchi is a scenic masterpiece

美しき　瀬戸内海を　庭にせし　ここ井ノ口は　絶景の地よ

Utsukushiki　Setonaikai o　niwa ni seshi
koko Inokuchi wa　zekkei no chi yo

❀

An island dim in the morning mist
Many oyster boats float on the waves

朝もやに　かすめる島を　遠くみて　かき船あまた　波にうかぶも

Asamoya ni　kasumeru shima o　tooku mite
kakibune amata　nami ni ukabu mo

We visit Momijidani Park deep in the mountain
Clear stream flows down where mountain air prevails

山深く　紅葉谷公園　来て見れば　清流おちて　山気みちみつ

Yama fukaku　Momijidani Koen　kitemireba
seiryu ochite　sanke michimitsu

❁

My heart is purified by the mountain air
The time of autumn tints is the best I think

山の気に　うたれて心　清々し　紅葉の頃は　一入をと思ふ

Yama no ke ni　utarete kokoro　sugasugashi
momiji no koro wa　hitoshio to omou

❁

The path up the Iroha Slope
Winds through scenes of autumn tints all over the mountain

いろは坂　のぼりゆく道　紅葉の　山一ぱいの　びょうぶ折れゆく

Irohazaka　noboriyuku michi　koyo no
yama ippai no　byobu oreyuku

We arrive at Shuzenji, a riverside inn
Our beds we spread side by side as we used to do at the dormitory

修善寺の　川辺にたてる　宿に来て　寄宿舎の如　床を並べぬ

Shuzenji no　kawabe ni tateru　yado ni kite
kishukusha no goto　toko o narabenu

Chapter 12
In Memory of Kurenai

Chapter 12 – In Memory of Kurenai

The following are poems written by members of the Ginushisha Poetry Club in honor of Kurenai Tsuneko Hongo.

❀

Praise Kurenai
She has accomplished all of her desires before her passing
I applaud her lifelong desire of creating poetry

己が身の　希いを果し　生涯を　歌詠み逝きし　人をたたえん

Onoga mi no　negai o hatashi　shogai o
uta yomiyukishi　hito o tataen
- By Reiko Kimoto

❀

Kurenai, whose death everyone mourned
She was the same age as myself, 78 years

惜まれて　逝きし紅　女史とわれ　同年輩の　七十八歳

Oshimarete　yukishi Kurenai　joshi to ware
donenpai no　shichijuhassai
- By Chokichi Okubo

I feel very closely connected to you as I read your poems to myself
Even though you have passed on

なつかしき　歌で結びし　友逝きて　一人かなしく　友の歌よむ

Natsukashiki　uta de musubishi　tomo yukite
hitori kanashiku　tomo no uta yomu
- By Mitsuyo Makinodan

❀

Your poems about today's world inspired people
Now I grieve Kurenai's death

うつし世を　詠みて歌いて　みちびきし　紅女史の　逝くぞかなしき

Utsushiyo o　yomite utaite　michibikishi
Kurenai-joshi no　yuku zo kanashiki
- By Matsuo Marutani

❀

As the sun sets on life, and my activities became limited
I look forward to only reading her poetry

老いの身に　暮れゆく日日の　親しみは　遺せし歌に　心こめつつ

Oi no mi ni　kureyuku hibi no　shitashimi wa
nokoseshi uta ni　kokorokometsutsu
- By Minokichi Oshiro

Chapter 12 – In Memory of Kurenai

As a crimson flower {Kurenai} fades in color
I lament her ascension as she has departed for an eternal voyage

紅の花　色あせて　永遠の　旅に出でたり　昇天悼む

Kurenai no hana   iroasete   eien no
tabi ni idetari   shoten itamu
- By Masayoshi Imai

❀

My friend was selected by god to pass
This evening I sorrowfully hear the hymns

我が友は　神に召されて　逝き給ふ　今宵聞こゆる　讃美歌悲し

Waga tomo wa   kami ni mesarete   yukitamou
koyoi kikoyuru   sanbika kanashi
- By Hisako Hirai

❀

Within the Hawaii Poetry Club
Kurenai planted the seeds for a beautiful poetry garden

紅女　ハワイ歌壇に　香の高き　実をば蒔き終へ　召されて逝きぬ

Kurenaijo   Hawai kadan ni   ka no takaki
mi o ba makioe   mesareteyukinu
- By Motoi Shioya

I had you write a poem about the tanzaku[24] even though you refused
This poem has become a memento

拒まれつつ　強いて書かせし　短冊の　歌こそ今は　形見なりけり

Kobamaretsutsu　shiite kakaseshi　tanzaku no
uta koso ima wa　kataminarikeri
- By Tetsuo Yukawa

❀

White chrysanthemum nests on your alter
In front of it people gather in your memory

白菊の　すがすがしきが　供へあり　紅女史を　悼む集り

Shiragiku no　sugasugashiki ga　sonaeari
Kurenai-joshi o　itamu atsumari
- By Saburo Higa

❀

You have left many poems for us
I hope Kurenai Hongo you pass peacefully into the next world

詠草を　数多残して　惜しまれる　紅本郷の　冥福祈る

Eiso o　amata nokoshite　oshimareru
Kurenai Hongo no　meifuku inoru
- By Norio Uehara (Tokuo)

---

[24] A long piece of paper on which poetry is written and is hung from a pole or bell clapper

Chapter 12 – In Memory of Kurenai

You left many poems for us
Lady Kureai may your soul rest peacefully

すぐれたる　歌の数々　残りゆく　紅女史の　魂安らかに

Suguretaru　uta no kazukazu　nokoriyuku
Kurenai-joshi no　tamashii yasurakani
- By Masao Murai

❀

"Shu yo tomo ni yadori mase" everyone sings
I hope your soul hears

「主よともに　宿りませ」と　和し歌う　讃歌をみ霊　聞き給へかし

"Shu yo tomo ni　yadori mase" to　washi utau
sanka o mitama kikitamaekashi
- By Masakazu Koide

❀

You have created many poems for us
I still can imagine your lovely figure

数々の　歌を残して　逝きませる　人の笑顔を　思いえがきぬ

Kazukazu no　uta o nokoshite　yukimaseru
hito no egao o　omoiegakinu
- By Kazuko Shimizu

I can hear your voice and also see your face
Have you really passed away?

声きこゆ　面又みゆる　哀れ君　君はまことに　逝きたまひしか

Koe kikoyu omo　mata miyuru　aware kimi
kimi wa makotoni　yukitamaishi ka
- By Junpei Fujima

❀

The red flower (Kurenai) has fallen forever
Although you have left many poems in this world

紅の 花は　果敢なく　散りにけり　歌の数々　此の世に残して

Kurenai no hana wa　hakanaku　chirinikeri
uta no kazukazu　kono yo ni nokoshite
- By Tsuneji Takami

❀

Good memories entered my mind
This evening while I read Lady Hongo's poems

なつかしき　想ひ湧くなり　今宵又　本郷姉の　歌を読みつつ

Natsukashiki　omoi wakunari　koyoi mata
Hongo-ane no　uta o yomitsutsu
- By Yoshiko Ota

Chapter 12 – In Memory of Kurenai

**Before we knew each other in our poetry group
You left us, now I grieved over the news of her death**

歌会の　同志の顔も　知らぬ間に　一人の訃報　受けて悲しむ

Utakai no　doshi no kao mo　shiranu ma ni
hitori no fuho　ukete kanashimu
- By Hashiji Kakazu

❀

**In heaven poetry groups continue
Please continue to write poetry, my poet friend**

天国にて　歌の集ひを　持たれかし　詠み続けてよ　歌の我が友

Tengoku ni te　uta no tsudoi o　motarekashi
yomitsuzukete yo　uta no waga tomo
- By Zenko Matayoshi

❀

**My dear friend, since you went to heaven
I realized the meaning of life is endless and infinite**

人生の　果敢なき深く　示されぬ　親しき君が　召されし日より

Jinsei no　hakanaki fukaku　shimesarenu
shitashiki kimi ga　mesareshi hi yori
- By Yoshiko Ide

My dear friend and also my dear teacher
I feel emptiness after you passed away

歌の友　我師と思ふ　其の方の　逝かれし後の　心淋しき

Uta no tomo　waga shi to omou　sono kata no
yukareshi nochi no　kokoro sabishiki
- By Tokie Kihara

❀

Creating poems in the rainy city[25] *about her friends and Musashino*
The poet Kurenai, you passed away

友を恋ひ　武蔵野恋ひて　雨降る町に　詠ひて逝きし　歌人紅

Tomo o koi　Musashino koite　ame furu machi ni
utaiteyukishi　Kajin-Kurenai
- By Katsuichi Yamada

❀

Reading Kurenai's poems are like beautiful glowing crimson color
I can not forget the beauty of my late friend

紅に　もゆる美しき　歌を詠みし　亡き友の温容　忘れ難きも

Kurenai ni　moyuru utsukushiki　uta o yomishi
naki tomo no onyo　wasuregatakimo
- By Yoshiko Kamiesu

---

[25] Hilo's rainfall is 130 inches/year

Chapter 12 – In Memory of Kurenai

Postscript

About Kurenai Tsuneko Hongo, Her Family, and Her Ancestors

About Kurenai Tsuneko Hongo

Kurenai Tsuneko Hongo

I was born at 27 Nishinaka-machi Asakusa-ku, Tokyo, Japan on January 25th, 1890.

My great grandfather became a Christian in the first year of Meiji (1868). He found great Christian joy in giving care through medical service to the people living in the Tokyo slums. In this way his faith had been fulfilled each day.

To live close to the slum district he moved to Asakusa, one of the most dense slum areas.

He was also appointed to give vaccinations to the Royal Family, but when an honor of a certain rank was bestowed on him, he declined it because of his modesty. His greatest honor and pleasure was to serve God and man through his profession.

Since then, because of Great Grandfather, the family embraced Christianity.

My grandfather's last words on his deathbed–"I can hear the angels' trumpets hallowing my homecoming." I was so moved and impressed, that soon after, in autumn, my decision was made. This led to my baptism when I was fourteen years old.

After my baptism by Rev. Thomson at Meisei Church Shitaya- ku Takemachi, I was sent to a Mission School, the Aoyama Institute where I was to have religious education. Notwithstanding the many years of strict and thorough Christian discipline, my stubborn nature often suffered my soul to stumble and bleed all over. Nevertheless the loving God has never let me down but has helped me and encouraged me to this day. Words cannot express my deep gratitude. Only with my Christian friends' loving care and God's strong hands, could I survive this life. Hymn 11 is my prayer and wish of every hour I live.

When the time comes to die, my soul is resurrected but my flesh is dead. After you have said farewell, please cremate my remains as soon as possible and if you need to have a service hold it in the evening at a church at your convenience and please no flowers. As my soul is at our father's side, I hope not to trouble you any more.

I would prefer simply a prayer at the Homelani Columbarium...

Tetsuo Yukawa
(Her Poetry and Church Friend)

The great grandfather Shosai Ono whom Kurenai mentions in her writing is said to have been a man of enlightened spirit. In that nationally isolated period of Japanese history, Shosai went to Nagasaki, the only port city open to the outside world then, to study Dutch for his medical studies.

At the dawn of a new age in Japan, suffering adversity, he fought against oppression and managed to break new ground by offering vaccinations. It is proper for a person, such as Shosai who had the entree of the Imperial household (Tenno ke), to have been recognized as one of the distinguished citizens with the others at this period of the Meiji era.

However, being a good Christian, he only served God and mankind, giving his whole life to the inhabitants of the slums he befriended. In those days the Christian religion was the object of general aversion. Moreover he gave no heed to worldly honor or wealth. I regret that his name had not been handed down to posterity despite his great service to humanity.

Kurenai's grandfather, Tsunenori Ono, was also a Christian of great faith. Through the influence of her grandfather she entered Aoyama Institute and became a Christian in her youth.

Her father who died when Kurenai was still very young is not fully known. Her mother's second marriage to Dr Tozaburo Niidate had given Kurenai two younger brothers and a sister. Therefore she is the third generation as a Christian.

In her early twenties on August 9, 1911, she sailed across to Hawaii. In 1912 and the next year she taught at *Honomu Institute* on the Big Island of Hawaii.

The head master of that prosperous institute was Rev. Shiro Sogabe, a great personality whom she respected with great reverence and affection. She often visited Rev. Shiro Sogabe in his old age to comfort and console him. Their relationship of teacher and pupil lasted all through the years and she watched over him beside his deathbed until the last moment.

On January 30, 1914 she was married to Torakiyo Hongo at Hilo Church. They were blessed with five sons and three daughters.

Under the pen name of "Kurenai" she had been writing poems heartily since her young days, but there was a break while bringing up her children and keeping house.

Postscript – About Kurenai Tsuneko Hongo

It was after the Hongos had entrusted their prosperous flower-culture and export business to their sons that Kurenai took up her poetry once again. Living in comfortable retirement she was seldom absent from the poetry meetings and she enjoyed writing poems from the bottom of her heart.

She attended not only the Ginushisha in her district but she also attended the poetry meetings in Honolulu. You could understand how great her enthusiasm for poetry was.

Even when she was stricken with that malignant disease, suffering from paralysis of her vocal cords, she wrote to me from her sick bed.

"I am grateful that I can still write though I have lost my speech."

How moving it was.

Meanwhile her illness worsened.

At last on November 20, 1968, she passed away at Kuakini Hospital. She was seventy-eight years old.

"All flesh is like grass and all its glory like the flower of the grass. The grass withers and the bloom drops off, but the word of the Lord endures forever."

This is a verse from The Bible. I Peter 1: 24, 25.

Kurenai left many poems, and with faith to her journey's end, she went back to her heavenly home! How blessed she was!

Torakiyo Hongo
(Kurenai's Husband)

We were able to bring out this little book by the generosity of Mr. Tetsuo Yukawa and friends of the deceased.

I trust that my wife did her best to fulfill her vocation through her long Christian life. In her daily life she took great interest in poetry and left many of her poems behind. This posthumous poem collection was selected from her notebooks.

May I express my gratitude to those who would kindly remember her through this little book.

"The Petals of the Vanda," the title of this book was taken from one of our flower-cultures.

During this book's production, I visited Japan and happened to find the reference to the records of her great grandfather Ono Shosai and grandfather Ono Tsunenori. It will be found in the postscript on the following pages.

About Shosai Ono
Kurenai's Great Grandfather
Hikotaro Umesawa, January 25, 1937

Dr Shosai Ono was born in April 17, 1819, in Dewa Akita prefecture. Doctor Ono studied medicine under Saito, the clan doctor, then under Ryotei Niimiya in Kyoto. He came to Edo, the present day Tokyo. He became a student to Seiken Tsuboi and studied under him for ten years.

After the service training was over, he settled down in Asakusa. He campaigned to encourage the use of vaccinations to prevent diseases. He is remembered as one of the great benefactors in the history of the use of vaccination in Japan.

The vaccinations he conducted counted to 23,000 people ranking from Emperor Taisho, who was then the crown prince Akemiya; the Empress Dowager Shoken, princes and princesses of the Royal family and other noble households of the upper class.

He fought from morning until night crusading to prevent small pox amongst the middle class and common people in downtown districts. We should truly thank him for what he did for our benefit.

Dr. Shosai Ono died July 17, 1888 at the age of seventy.

About Tsunenori Ono
Kurenai's Grandfather
Tokuko Ono
(Kurenai's mother)

My father is from Dr. Shunkai of Sakura Juntendo family and came to my mother's family to marry her. His former name was Shoan Honbashi. By this marriage his name changed to Tsunenori Ono.

He had a position in the military service from which he resigned because the Ono clinic became so busy and needed his help. He was a first grade army doctor and was honored with the senior grade of the seventh Court rank.

He hoped to resign at the rank of surgeon major-colonel, but my grandfather requested him to resign and made my father assist him. My father was the vaccinator to Emperor Meiji's two grandsons.

The Imperial household sent a coach for him on such occasions. Mr. Tsunatsune Hashimoto assisted my father in holding the tray when he vaccinated the royal family.

Six months later my father died on April 28, 1903.

Dr. Teijiro Watanabe was one of my father's pupils.

Dr. Suke Yamazaki
(Lecturer at the former Imperial University)

Dr. Tsunenori Ono must have been a man of great personality.

His career is mentioned in the "Medical Magazine" by Dr. Nobuyoshi Tsuboi published in 1874, November, No. 7 issue.

The writer is Yoshie Hayashi under the title of "Controversy on Cowpox Vaccination." The head of the medical office, Dr.Jun Matsumoto entrusted the preservation of cowpox seedling-bed to the Ono clinic.

By his father-in-law's order, Dr. Ono devoted his services for those purposes through the war periods of the Meiji Era. He received fifty koku when the vaccination building was constructed.

In 1881, December, he was appointed to the health bureau in the Ministry of Home Affairs. His office was Superintendent of the Shitaya Vaccinia Lab Institute.

During this period he held conferences with Dr. Matsumoto on the development of vaccinations. For his good services, he was awarded the senior grade of the seventh Court rank in 1884.

Then he resigned from government service and succeeded to his father-in-law's profession as vaccinator to the public.

The Ono Family Tree

The ancestors of the Ono family lived as country samurai in Echizen-no-kuni, the present Fukui Prefecture, at Onogun, along the Ono river ridge. They belonged to the Heishi family so they had to escape beyond the reach of the Genji family, who became the conqueror of that region.

The Ono family fled north up to Shonai in Dewa, the present Akita Prefecture.

They opened an inn for ship passengers patronized under the Akita clan at Akita port. At the same time they ran a sake brewery under the name of Nebuya Yoemon.

A Timeline for Kurenai

1890	January 25	Born at Nishinakamachi, Asakusa-ku, Tokyo
1904	Fall	Baptized by Rev Thompson at Myojo Church, Ake-cho, Shitaya-ku, Tokyo
1908	March	Graduated from Aoyama Institute
1911	August 9	Sailed to Hawaii
1912-13		Instructor at Hanomu private school in Hawaiian Island
1914	January 10	Married Torakiyo Hongo at Hilo Church
1968	November 20	Died at Kuakini Hospital in Honolulu at the age of seventy-eight.

Family Tree

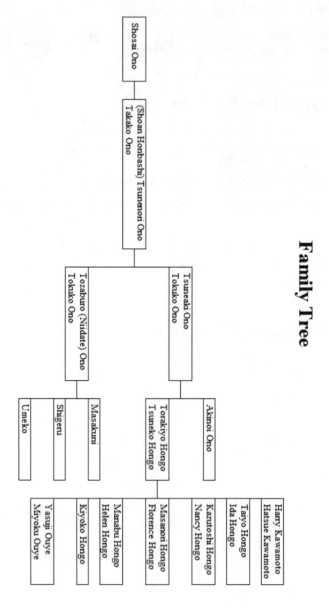

Shosai Ono

(Shoan Honbashi) Tsunenori Ono
Takako Ono

Tsuneaki Ono
Tokuko Ono

Tozaburo (Niidate) Ono
Tokuko Ono

Torakiyo Hongo
Tsuneko Hongo

Akinoi Ono

Masakuni

Shigeru

Umeko

Masanori Hongo
Florence Hongo

Kazutoshi Hongo
Nancy Hongo

Taiyo Hongo
Ida Hongo

Harry Kawamoto
Hatsue Kawamoto

Manabu Hongo
Helen Hongo

Kiyoko Hongo

Yasuji Ouye
Miyoku Ouye

Acknowledgements and Credits

The Creators of *Vanda no Hanabira*

Ginushisha Poetry Club - Zenko Matayoshi and Tetsuo Yukawa

The Initial Project Team for *Petals of the Vanda*

The late *Hatsue Hongo Kawamoto* (daughter) - project coordinator and lead

The late *Shizue Helen Oka* (niece) – initial translator of "*Vanda no Hanabira*"

Audrey Hongo Adachi (granddaughter) – transcriber of the handwritten translation

Jon Noel Yoshiwara – transcriber to computer format

Florence Hongo (daughter-in-law) – editor and book consultant

The Nagaishi family – transcribers of the Japanese text and calligrapher for the front cover

Kay Hironaka – watercolor paintings of the vanda orchids

Janice Hongo Avellana (granddaughter) – the initial book designer

The Final Project Team for *Petals of the Vanda*

Masanori Hongo (son) – project coordinator, executive editor, translator, and writer

Miyako Sueyoshi – translation editor

Leonard Chan – editor, book layout, and cover photo

Philip Chin – editor

Jean Chan – cover and incidental art designer

Harry Kawamoto (son-in-law & husband of *Hatsue Hongo Kawamoto*) – financial and general benefactor

Special Thanks

Garrett Hongo (grand-nephew) – for reading the book and contributing the foreward

Margo King Lenson – for reading the book and supplying us with a review

Theresa Tong, Sharon Chan, & Kim Yoshiwara – for reviewing the book and for the edit suggestions

O for a Heart to Praise my God
Kurenai's Favorite Hymnal

Translated into English by *Charles Wesley and Thomas Haweis*

O for a heart to praise my God,
A heart from sin set free,
A heart that always feels, Thy blood
So freely shed for me!

A humble, lowly, contrite heart,
Believing, true and clean,
Which neither life nor death can part
From Him that dwells within.

A heart in every thought renewed,
And full of love divine;
Perfect and right and pure and good,
A copy, Lord, of Thine!

Ametsuchi ni masaru kami no mina o
Homuru ni taru beki kokoro mo gana

Ogorazu terawazu herikudarite
Waga Shu no mikura to narase tamae

Ikurumo shinurumo tada Shu o omou
Yuruganu kokoro o atae tamae

Kokoro o kiyomete ai o mitashi
Waga Shu no misugata narase tamae

Mimegumi yutakeki Shu yo kitarite
Kokoro ni mina o ba shirushi tamae